UNIVERSITY OF MINNESOTA

P9-DFC-695

Wright Morris

BY LEON HOWARD

813.
52
MORRIS
How

FINKELSTEIN
MEMORIAL LIBRARY
SPRING VALLEY, N. Y.

UNIVERSITY OF MINNESOTA PRESS · MINNEAPOLIS

860184 PAPER

© Copyright 1968 by the University of Minnesota

ALL RIGHTS RESERVED

Printed in the United States of America at
the North Central Publishing Company, St. Paul

Library of Congress Catalog Card Number: 68-64752

PUBLISHED IN GREAT BRITAIN, INDIA, AND PAKISTAN BY THE OXFORD
UNIVERSITY PRESS, LONDON, BOMBAY, AND KARACHI, AND IN CANADA
BY THE COPP CLARK PUBLISHING CO. LIMITED, TORONTO

WRIGHT MORRIS

LEON HOWARD is a professor of English at the University of California, Los Angeles, and the author of a history of American literature and books on Herman Melville, James Russell Lowell, Jonathan Edwards, and the Connecticut Wits.

↙ *Wright Morris*

WRIGHT MORRIS has been the most consistently original of American novelists for a quarter of a century which has borne witness to his originality by refusing to keep his novels in print. Faulkner once occupied the same position, though not for so long a time; and Morris' longer stay may have been his own fault, as Leslie Fiedler once remarked, because he would never join a gang. Perhaps he could not because he had anticipated and discounted too many of them. He discovered early that life, from any rational point of view, was absurd but took the discovery as a matter of fact rather than as a revelation of philosophical truth. He developed a sympathy for common humanity and an eye and ear for its peculiarities without becoming an alienated or angry young man. He realized that the American archetype of the self-sufficient hero was inappropriate to the modern world and simply avoided the traditional character instead of preserving the cliché with an "anti-hero" or some other man of straw. He lit out for the Territory, in the words of Huck Finn, ahead of the rest and made it, in his own play on the words, a territory in time rather than in space. Because of this he may prove to be not only the most original but the most important American novelist of the mid-century.

But for that reason, too, he is difficult to represent, justly, in any succinct account of his work. The charm that he exercises over his occasional readers is that of wit, humor, and vividness in his presentation of ordinary people who somehow become extraordinary under his touch; and his consistent followers are fascinated by the extraordinary range and depth of his human understanding. A great variety of midwestern, eastern, far western, and southern Americans appear in his novels, and so do French, Germans, Austrians, Italians, Greeks, and Mexicans of all sorts — all of them believably and amusingly human. No other American novelist has approached him in the rich variety of his raw materials and in the ability to keep them raw enough to seem real while they are being handled with an art as sophisticated as that of Henry James. The range of Morris' work cannot be separated from its texture; and any figure in the carpet must be sought beneath the realistic depth and comic surface of the nap.

Although Morris writes from experiences with which he is deeply concerned, the figure is not autobiographical. The chief facts of his life are quickly told: He was born in Central City, Nebraska, on January 6, 1910, and lived with his father in various small Nebraska towns and in Omaha before moving to Chicago in 1924. He entered Pomona College in 1930, after several months on the Texas ranch of his Uncle Dwight Osborn. Withdrawing from college in 1933, he spent a year in France, Germany, Austria, and Italy, and then settled in California and began writing. During the summers of 1938 and 1939 he lived in Wellfleet, Massachusetts, where he developed the interest in photography that he cultivated and turned to professional use on a long tour of the United States in 1940–41 and on two later trips to his native Nebraska. He lived in Pennsylvania from 1944 until 1954, when he began spending much of his time abroad — especially in Mexico, Venice, and Greece — and in California. Since 1963 he has been teaching at San Francisco State College and living in Mill Valley. Many incidents that appear in Morris' books — some with annoying repetition — are obviously loosely related to one or another of these periods in his life. But his usable experiences have been of the sort that he could reshape freely in his imagination or else they have been like Wordsworthian "spots of time" which nourished his mind and created inward agitations. And the serious autobiographical element in his work comes from his constant concern, while writing, with the relationship between the identifiable past and the unknown future and with the part the artist plays in clarifying it.

The first two of his novels were exploratory in their attempt to discover a point of view which would enable him to handle material in which he was emotionally involved with a detachment that would control any impulse he might have to base art on emotion. *My Uncle Dudley* (1942) was perhaps more fully drawn from personal experience than any novel he was to write later. Its cast of characters consisted of eight men, a boy, and a second-hand Marmon automobile; and its plot was a comic odyssey of misadventure from the lotus land of southern California, through the mountains of Arizona, and across the plains to the flooded banks of the Mississippi. The trip was one Morris had made with his father in the spring of 1927, but the most important single episode in the book (an arbitrary arrest and a bad night in a Mississippi jail) was based upon an experience only a few months old and still fresh in the author's mind at the time the book was written. The passengers and the jail episode were both skillfully used to bring out the character of Uncle Dudley, whose ridiculous pear-shaped figure and successful operations as a confidence man did not prevent him from living up to his proverbial and even mythological name — he was every boy's "Uncle Dudley" to whom he could tell anything and expect understanding, sympathy, and wisdom in return. He was also a wily and audacious Ulysses, and his final gesture of audacity — in a completely invented scene — fulfills the somewhat obscure fictional promise of the earlier incidents and gives meaning to the book.

The theme of audacity, often highly eccentric, was to become

7

an important one in Morris' novels. Quite early, here, Dudley had described himself as a "horseless knight" who had once thought he was meant "to ride up front and holler and point at the promised land." But now, disillusioned by the realization that there was no one dream good for all the people, he found that he had acquired more armor than a man should need but had found no horse to mount. Later, in the Mississippi jail, he discovered a man who professed to be "a dam good horse" — Furman, recognized by the inmates as the best man in the jail, who was regularly put there for spitting in a cop's eye and who unconsciously parodied Tom Paine by insisting that his place had "come to be wherever such basterds is." Furman had spat on every officer except the sadistic Cupid; and when Uncle Dudley was released on the roadside, ill and exhausted by his experiences, he somehow found the spirit to mount Furman's hobby: chewing his cigar into brown juice, he laughed as gaily as he had ever laughed and spat Cupid squarely in the eye. He was dragged back into the police car and to whatever sadistic punishment awaited him, and the narrator's last view was of the car swinging into town with his Uncle Dudley's arm out gallantly signaling the turn.

The audacity of Uncle Dudley's performance, however, is more significant in the light of Morris' later uses of the theme than it might have appeared to be in this first novel. Of more immediate importance was Morris' effort to solve the technical problem of achieving sufficient detachment from his material to avoid being dominated by it. He did so by using an adolescent narrator known only as the Kid — one of the many kid storytellers who appear to have composed a substantial portion of American literature. But Morris' adolescent was not a persona (as were the comparable narrators in Mark Twain, Sherwood Anderson, Hemingway, and Faulkner) whose verbal limitations enabled the author to escape conventionality or triteness in the communication of emotion. He was a sound-camera which recorded no emotion at all. He enabled the author to appear completely detached from the experiences recorded in the book — to appear in the role of T. S. Eliot's artist as a catalytic agent or in the role of Hughes Mearns's haunting "man who wasn't there."

Yet Morris was unable to accept Eliot's fantasy of the artist as "a bit of finely filiated platinum," and the reality of the artist's existence, both as a human being and as a catalytic agent, became the subject of his next book. *The Man Who Was There* (1945) was concerned with a character who makes his presence felt through his absence: he is "there" not as a person but as a personality as well as a catalytic agent whose brief associations with the characters in the novel expand their notions of their own experience. Agee Ward has gone to war and been reported missing in action, and the novel deals with his actual past and the present he has achieved in the minds of those who knew him — such remarkable characters as Grandmother Herkimer and Private Reagan in the first section and the Spavics, Mrs. Krickbaum, Gussie Newcomb, and Mr. Bloom in the third. The Agee Ward remembered in the first section was a younger version of the Kid, that in the last was an incipient Uncle Dudley. He had gone to war, according to Mrs. Krickbaum, because of his concern for "the human predicament": he "didn't like it, but he was in it" and "Bad as it is, he said, we had to keep it *hu*-man!" In effect, he did, and made it comic as well. Morris left no doubt of his belief that a man — portrayed as an artist in this instance — could be "there" in the sense that he was a cause which had a humanizing effect upon a future of which he was not and could not be aware.

This belief and the characters used to reveal it were to prove prophetic of a long line of development in Morris' fiction. Another line was foreshadowed in the middle section which he called "The Three Agee Wards" and in which he anticipated the photo-text technique and the substance of his next two books. The first Agee Ward was presented through the medium of "The Album" which contained descriptions of real and imaginary family photographs (some of them to be reproduced later in *The Home Place*) and of drawings and correspondence of the sort Morris himself might have sent a friend during his travels in Europe. The second was introduced in "The Ward Line" which was factually based on Morris' return to Nebraska in the days of the Dust Bowl and the discovery of his father's surviving relatives. And the other was identified by the village barber who recognized "The Osborn Look" and knew that he was "there," in the person of his mother, thirty years before. Time was almost an illusion before the barber's sense of human continuity. And so was space. "Where you're goin' is where you're from," he said; and with these casual words he attributed to man that transient and ephemeral position in time and space which was to haunt Morris' imagination for the next twenty years.

His next three books were primarily concerned with the problem of man's identity in time and space, and for them he developed a medium which made artistic use of the stability of vision and the suggestiveness of words. His earlier use of the Kid as a sound-camera had the disadvantage of keeping the lens and the microphone together; and the device of the Album in *The Man Who Was There*, while separating the two, obscured the distinction by requiring a verbal representation of the picture. His new medium was a combination of photographs with a text to which they bore a suggestive rather than illustrative relationship.

His first experiment with the method, in *The Inhabitants* (1946), was much too ambitious because it was an attempt at the admittedly impossible — to show "what it is to be an American." It was impossible because Morris shared (and repeated) Uncle

Dudley's conviction that "there's no one thing to cover the people, no one sky . . . no one dream." But he could seek out "the inhabitants," from New England to California, and let the photographs show the houses people grew up in (either to keep or to leave) and let the people themselves talk or think aloud in the complementary prose text. The houses and the people were both "inhabitants." For Morris, while photographing an architectural quality of the sort that Thoreau said grew "from within outward, out of the necessities and character of the indweller," insisted that each man was himself "inhabited" by what he had grown up in. And he made use of this idea in his photographs when he subtly suggested a continuity in the "uncoverable" American experience by tracing the survival of New England architectural decoration through the porches of the Midwest and Colorado mining towns until it culminated in a desolate and windowless adobe house with a classic Yankee door lintel.

Although *The Inhabitants* attempted too much (especially for a volume of only slightly more than a hundred pages) it anticipated several books to come, particularly *The Home Place* (1948) in which Morris undertook an intensely personal exploration of the early background that "inhabited" him and, through him, so many of his books. More conventional than *The Inhabitants*, it modified the purely suggestive or poetic relationship between text and photographs and was something that might be considered an extra-illustrated novel. But the photographs are primary and the story obviously designed for a less sophisticated understanding than *The Inhabitants* demanded. In it the character who had once been Agee Ward was transformed into Clyde Muncy (though still an Osborn on his mother's side), a writer with a wife and two children who were refugees from the housing shortage in New York and were returning to the Muncy home place near Lone Tree, Nebraska, with some hope of finding a place to live in.

While they were visiting the aging Uncle Harry and Aunt Clara the convenient death of Uncle Ed made available the house across the road. It had been promised to Cousin Ivy, who would farm Uncle Harry's eighty acres; but their need superseded Ivy's, and they would have had the place if the wife, Peggy, had not discovered what Morris observed in *The Inhabitants*: "I've never been in anything so crowded, so full of something, as the rooms of a vacant house." They move on instead.

The story of *The Home Place* is contrived but the "spots of time" captured in the narrative make this book crucial to an understanding of all Morris' Nebraska novels and several of the others. Here is the explanation of the problem Agee Ward has with the difference between kinesthetic and pictorial memory: the pump, which seemed so far away when he was a small boy carrying water, was as close to the house as he saw it in his mind's eye. Here in pictures are the objects which so many of Morris' characters share as childhood memories: the Model T Ford, the corncob stove, the rusty tractor, the solitary egg, the outdoor privy, and the old wooden grain elevator in which two small boys might hide and peek out to see the world end. Everything was old and worn out. The drought and dust storms of the thirties had killed the trees, weathered the buildings, and withered the people. One can easily see, looking through *The Home Place*, why Morris had difficulty in distinguishing between nostalgia and nausea in his attitude toward Nebraska. When he returned and photographed these early scenes and artifacts, he found it a place to be from rather than to be in, but not a place to forget. The people who had not gone away had endured hardships that made men. Their memories were long, and such returned natives as Agee Ward and Clyde Muncy found themselves more real as memories than they were as persons.

In *The World in the Attic* (1949) — a sequel to *The Home Place*, though published without photographs — the Muncy family has moved on from Lone Tree to the town of Junction, where Clyde's mother's family had lived and where his father had been the station agent for the Chicago, Burlington, and Quincy railroad. Stopping for a bite to eat and to see Clyde's old school friend, Bud Hibbard, they spend the night and Clyde opens a door into a Nebraska which has something in common with Faulkner's Mississippi. It is the world of Bud's grandmother, "Aunt Angie," who inhabits the kitchen and basement of the big house built by her son Clinton for his bride, imported from the Deep South and known to the children of Clyde's generation as "Miss Caddy." Upon Clinton's death, Aunt Angie had sealed her domain and settled down in a tough determination to outlive her daughter-in-law, who had retired into the even more private world of her upstairs bedroom (the "attic" of the title). She does, though no one is sure that her wandering mind is aware of it until she makes her grotesque appearance, through the long-sealed door, at the funeral.

The Home Place marked the climax of Morris' search for identity through the discovery of the past which "inhabited" him and gave him the individual character he was always to maintain. He accepted his destiny as a midwestern novelist as completely as Faulkner accepted his as a southern one. As a writer he kept going to where he was from. But the Midwest to which he had returned at the end of the Dust Bowl era was a static world in the attic which he refused to abide in. If the West had declined instead of advancing with the twentieth century, he would explore the East — though not without nostalgia for the masculine world of his childhood. But he took with him, in his imagination, several characters from *The World in the Attic*: one husband with his conviction that he was married to "the finest creature on God's green earth," another with his tendency to withdraw into his own affairs and accept his home as his wife's domain, and a strong-minded eccentric old grandmother. What would happen to them in the eastern Eden which had not been devastated by dust and decay?

The first two novels of Morris' new exploration — *Man and Boy* (1951) and *The Works of Love* (1952) — were closely inter-twined in conception and in composition. In the rather slight *Man and Boy* the story deals with the events of a single day before the end of World War II. The Boy has died heroically, and the Navy is to name a destroyer in his honor. Mother rises to the occasion in her own inimitable way while her husband Warren merely goes along as the man who hides from her whims when he can, yields to them when he must, and remembers the Boy as a youngster to whom he had given an air rifle which caused the bird-loving Mother to abolish Christmas forevermore and the Boy to assert himself as a hunter and perhaps inevitably seek his final escape by death in action.

The book was suggested by a real occurrence and by Morris' amused but fascinated view of the eccentricities of a real man-aging female, but it developed imaginatively out of his effort to understand the control such a woman could have over the fallen race of man. "Mother" — Mrs. Violet Ames Ormsby — was not only the central character but the heroine of the book, who could ride roughshod over United States Navy protocol as readily as she could over the weak-willed Mr. Ormsby or the Boy, Virgil, who was "there" in such different ways to his two parents. Rather curiously Morris attributed her discovery of the value of aggres-siveness to an incident which was a part of his own experience and which he was to develop more fully in a short story, "The Rites of Spring" — a visit to an Uncle Dwight's ranch in Texas, where she responded aggressively (as the narrator of the later piece did not) to the threat of a little boy who frightened her by his wild behavior with a piece of broken glass. He also drew upon his own experiences when he hinted at a background for Mr. Ormsby similar to that of the boy who was already beginning to evolve in *The Works of Love*. But the crucial character in Morris' search for an understanding of the spiritual Amazon was Private Lipido, a small soldier in a big helmet who joined the party to protect Mr. Ormsby from Mother, assaulted her dignity from behind, and was so overcome by his failure that by the end of the ceremony he was more attentive to her than Mr. Ormsby was. Mother did not owe her position to the weak "Momism" Philip Wylie was attributing to the American male at about the same time: there was strength of character and a basic dignity beneath her comic eccentricities.

The comedy of *Man and Boy* is almost perfectly balanced by the pathos of *The Works of Love* in which the central character, Will Brady, is the sort of man from whom Mr. Ormsby might have inherited his capacity for acceptance. Like Mr. Ormsby's father, he was a big egg man from the Midwest; and, though temporarily successful in business, he was helpless in his unbearable connections with women who were too insensitive to appreciate his humble and inarticulate works of love. There were four of them: the prostitute who laughed at his proposal of marriage, the prostitute who ran away and sent him another man's child to adopt, the hotel owner's widow who slept tightly wrapped in a sheet, and finally the cigar-counter girl — nearer in age to his adopted son — who ran away with a "Hawayan" and reappeared as an alcoholic streetwalker. There was also the boy whom he loved as Willy Brady, Jr., and tried pathetically to understand by reading *Tom Sawyer* and *Penrod*. Will's works of love, for these and others, consisted of a sensitive kindly benevolence; and when he had abandoned his business and his suburban house in

Omaha and drifted alone to Chicago, he got the sort of job he had symbolically earned — that of a department store Santa Claus — and a death he invited almost as he had always invited disappointment.

Will Brady's story is one of the most moving that Morris has ever told, because it is the story of a man who had a dream of unpretentious goodness which could not be fulfilled — or, as Uncle Dudley might have put it, the story of a man who had a gentle horse but was too gentle to ride it. The book is reminiscent of Sherwood Anderson and is partially dedicated to his memory as a "pioneer in the works of love." But Morris is closer to the Anderson who created the "grotesques" of *Winesburg, Ohio* and the earlier novels than to the Anderson who believed that a man who abandoned material success could find a better life: Will Brady could offer goodness, but he could find no one to accept it for what it was. The works of love were all on one side.

Morris worked longer on *The Works of Love* than on any of his earlier novels, beginning it nearly six years before he published the redaction of a much longer manuscript, and the book is rich in memories of his own adolescence and filled with allusions to the artifacts, spots of time, and individuals who appear in his other early books. It gives the impression of being an intensely personal novel with a fictitious plot created out of private feelings. A certain reserve seems particularly evident in his treatment of the women who play so important a part in Will Brady's one-sided life. All of them are self-centered, all are willing to exploit Will in their various ways, all are incapable of such peripheral works of love as understanding and tolerance, and all are somewhat unreal. Morris was able to present in sharp but not unappreciative caricature an aggressively callous type of female but not the merely insensitive kind, and in his next and perhaps best novel of this period he returned to a new version of Violet Ormsby and gave her a husband with more personality than he had allowed Mr. Ormsby and more force of character than he had attributed to Will Brady.

The Deep Sleep (1953) may, in fact, become a classic study of American family life. Judge Howard Porter has just died when the story opens, but he is very much a "man who was there" in the memory of Parsons (the hired man who knows more about the family than its members know about themselves) and in the mind of Paul Webb, the son-in-law who recalls the man he knew as a public figure and discovered as a private individual on the day before his funeral. The Judge had been a person of power and influence in the state, and Parsons had known him as a man to be deeply respected while Webb knew of the high regard for him among his associates in Philadelphia. But he had never been known at all by his mother (the eccentric "Grandmother" whose prototype had appeared as "Aunt Angie" in *The World in the Attic* and as Violet Ames's mother in *Man and Boy*) and was rarely "there" as a human being to his wife — only twice, within the testimony of the novel: once in Italy, five years after their wedding, when their marriage "sort of came to a point" and the first of his two children was conceived; and again at the end of a long day of preparations for the funeral, when she admitted to her daughter Katherine, "I'm going to miss your father." Katherine's own position in the novel is ambiguous. As a young girl she had decided to lead her own life instead of withdrawing into herself (as her brother, like Virgil Ormsby, did before he too was killed in the war), and as the wife of the artist Webb she had escaped into another world which enabled her to feel sorry for her parents' bondage to the petty routine of home life. But Morris allowed her to behave at times like her mother's daughter — as though he suspected that every woman is an Eve, born of man's deep sleep, and a potential instrument of his destruction.

The discoveries Paul Webb makes during the long day, however, cast a new light on the marital relationship of the Porters. The Judge had told Parsons that "Around the house . . . I leave it up to the Missus," but Webb uncovers evidence of the Judge's many small evasions of his wife's compulsion to keep everything under control. He learns of the shallow ford in the river where the Judge parked his car and pretended to be on an island, the basement toilet where he sat in darkness and knew that for twenty years a bottle of whiskey had been on hand in case of need, and the attic where he smoked cigars and kept the expensive Swiss watch he had bought to celebrate the high point of his marriage and had been required to put in "a safe place" after temporarily losing it on a bird-watching expedition. He had left all the responsibilities of the house to Parsons (who was in some respects closer to Mrs. Porter than he was), yet he was not, in any spiritual sense, withdrawn from his wife. He felt as surely as Parsons did that she was "a remarkable woman," and, dying, he insisted that her empty bed be drawn within reach of his hand because he didn't like to be alone. He cried out against his mother, but he clove to his wife even though she drove him to petty concealments which destroyed his dignity.

There is a certain mythological unity in these three novels of the early fifties: *Man and Boy* is a comic prelude to a drama of the fall of man. Showing man in his fallen state, it is appropriately staged in a bourgeois setting far removed from the Great Plains where man was dominant and woman merely endured. *The Works of Love* is a representation of the fall, which is synchronized with Will Brady's migration eastward and toward greater material prosperity until he was forced to give it up. And *The Deep Sleep* is Morris' attempt to justify the fall in the Miltonic sense of asserting that whatever passes for Providence in twentieth-century metaphysics is free from guilt. For there is no God in

Morris' imaginative universe — and no Satan, in the form either of a serpent or of a social system. Man falls, like Milton's angels, "self-tempted, self-depraved"; but he falls from the "single imperfection" Milton attributed to Man — a "deficience" within himself which was "the cause of his desire/ By conversation with his like to help/ Or solace his defects." Or, to put the explanation into terms closer to those Morris himself used, man needs challenge and love while woman wants security; and if he meets his challenge well enough to fall into the deep sleep of security, out of it will come the woman, bone of his bones and flesh of his flesh, who will tempt him to destruction through his works of love.

Within this imaginative pattern *The Huge Season* (1954), though a novel quite different in kind, may be seen as closely related to the others through Morris' continued concern with the mystery of Paradise lost. It is different in kind because most of its raw material is related to Morris' college days rather than to his earlier background or to his observations of the inhabitants of the "wild station wagon country" of the Pennsylvania Main Line and also because it is the first of his stories to be told from the single viewpoint of a fully characterized persona. The persona is Peter Foley, professor of classics in a small Pennsylvania college, whose memory operates on two distinct levels: One is that of his conscious attempt to recapture for a book the circumstances of a strange "captivity" he had experienced during his first two years in a small California college when he shared a dormitory suite with several young men, all of whom were iron filings in the field of a magnet provided by Charles Lawrence — a tennis player. The other is that of the free associations created by the events of a single day spent in New York after one of his suitemates, Jesse Proctor, had testified before the Senate Committee on Un-American Activities. They run together, at the end, when

Foley realizes that the captivity has been lifelong and that he has at last escaped.

The Huge Season is a haunting book because it deals with a form of human bondage more subtle than that portrayed in the trilogy on the fall of man. Yet the theme is the same, with much larger implications. Lawrence's determination to be a great tennis player, despite the handicap of one bad arm to begin with, represents the same irrational compulsiveness that is displayed by Mrs. Ormsby in her determination to live by platitudes and Mrs. Porter's obsession with keeping things in order even to the extent of hanging out used paper towels to dry. His more sensitive suitemates — Foley, Proctor, and to a lesser extent Lundgren — can only follow him and protect him where he is vulnerable. Lawrence was a man on a horse, as Uncle Dudley would have put it, but it was the compulsiveness of his horsemanship rather than the direction of his leadership which captivated the others against their wills.

The composition of *The Huge Season* appears to have been a turning point in Morris' literary development. The first of his novels to be focused upon a character (Lawrence) who was entirely a product of his imagination, it was also the first to end on a note — underplayed though it was — of assured freedom. A possible clue to the imaginative and emotional change reflected in it may be found in an odd and seemingly irrelevant passage halfway through the book. Foley's cat had brought home an apparently dead chipmunk, deposited it bottom side up on a flagstone, and given it a few casual cuffs. Then "the chipmunk sprang up like [a] spring-wind toy and began to dance . . . his little tail like a banner, hopping back and forth on the cool flagstone." The incident reoccurred day after day during the summer while the chipmunk got fat and Foley began to read Darwin and "spend nights brooding on a creative evolution of his own. Founded on what? Well, founded on audacity. The unpredictable behavior that lit up the darkness with something new. . . . Perhaps, Foley thought, Mother Nature was originating again. . . . Maybe she had come to feel, quite a bit like Foley, that she had played her cards wrong in the first place and that the time had come to put a few trial irons into the fire. . . . If what Nature had in mind was survival, Man had ceased to be at the heart of Nature and had gone off on a suicidal impulse of his own. And Foley's chipmunk, among others, had got wind of it."

Foley, later, during his day in New York, was to think of himself as "having come from no more than the glint in the eye of a chipmunk with nothing on its mind but a sublime audacity," and Morris himself was to continue to play with this fancy. He conceived of *The Field of Vision* (1956) in terms of the spectator's reaction to a bullfight in which the ring served as talisman attracting the "durable fragments of a man's life" and forcing him "to come to imaginative terms with them." Of his seven principal characters, he used five for his major purpose: McKee (a small-town Babbitt or older and more prosperous Bud Hibbard, who had just enough imagination to be held in captivity by a flamboyant boyhood friend), Lois (his wife, not as eccentric as Mrs. Ormsby or Mrs. Porter but as "stiffly laced into her corset of character"), Scanlon (Lois' father, the eighty-seven-year-old hermit of Lone Tree, an ex-plainsman who had seen the century turn but had failed to turn with it and was now only "the mummified effigy of the real thing"), Gordon Boyd (the boyhood friend, "the man who was there," who had been a sort of Lawrence in his youth but was now a professional hero, long unemployed, who could not even be a successful failure), and Dr. Lehmann (a Brooklynized German psychiatrist, who was almost as odd as the few patients who stayed with him). Two other characters were actively in the consciousness of the others, though Morris did not directly reveal their own: Gordon, McKee's eight-year-old grandson, an "infant Davy Crockett" who bore Boyd's name; and Paula Kahler, Lehmann's apparently simpleminded housekeeper and patient.

In exploring the durable fragments of the lives of his five characters, Morris achieved a range and depth that is to be found in none of his earlier novels. Scanlon, too blind to see where he was but aroused by the cry of *"agua"* when the matador's cape needed wetting down, returned completely to the past and a vivid recollection of the wagon train that lost most of its members from thirst as they crossed the Death Valley. Lois, who fainted and had to leave when a boy was almost gored, saw mostly Boyd and remembered the sexual awakening he had aroused with a kiss and she had suppressed by marrying McKee. McKee, who tried to see the fights but looked after Lois as a matter of course, remembered Boyd and his unsuccessful attempt to walk on water, his own youthful failure in courage, and the strange influence Boyd continued to exercise upon him. And Boyd, who saw more of the fights than the others, remembered Ty Cobb's pocket which as a boy he had torn off the pants of the great ballplayer and throughout his years of seedy decay had kept as a private talisman — a conjure-rag of dreams — and his only permanent possession.

All represented some aspect of fallen man — regression and withdrawal, repression, servitude, and failure — brilliantly presented in terms which kept the human condition human. The two characters who appeared to have fallen furthest from the human condition, however, represented something else. The half-clown and half-charlatan, Lehmann, could see the fights and also Paula at his side, quietly knitting and unaware of what was going on. He remembered her history. Born Paul, and gentle almost to saintliness in the opinion of the director of a Chicago YMCA, his patient had been discovered as a chambermaid in a Brooklyn hotel where she had strangled an amorous bellhop in an elevator and lapsed into complete placidity. By an act of imagination — "with nothing on its mind but a sublime audacity" — an individual had re-created itself, and Dr. Lehmann's mind had been audacious enough to come to imaginative terms with that fact. So, as with the chipmunk in *The Huge Season*: "In Leopold Lehmann the inscrutable impulse was reaching for the light. As it was in Paula Kahler. As it was in the species with the bubble at the top. But the thrust, even in reaching for the light, must come from behind. . . . In reaching for more light man would have to risk such light as he had. It was why he needed help. It was why he had emerged as man. It was according to his nature that he was obliged to exceed himself." The oddest of characters in Morris' field of vision represented the best odds he could see in favor of human evolution.

This evolution was not Darwinian. It was a modern version of the "reconciliation of science and poetry" which Joseph Le Conte had taught young Frank Norris two generations before and which has perhaps been best brought up to date by Loren Eiseley after he had spent days, with Morris, watching a real cat and a real chipmunk put on the performance described in *The Huge Season*. In writing of *The Field of Vision* Morris referred to the "unchanging drives" of the imagination (the less audacious Le Conte had called it "Divine energy" and Eiseley had called it "the human heart") and said that the book had grown from his belief that the "imaginative act is man himself." His later books were to be based upon this belief too — at least in the sense that their invention was affected by the change this belief made in Morris' aims as an artist. Henceforth he was to be concerned with coming to imaginative terms with the past less than with those forces which might affect the future.

23

Yet it was a reassertion of his belief in evolution that kept *Love among the Cannibals* (1957) in the mainstream of his literary development; otherwise it might well have slipped into that backwash of talent usually reflected in the Hollywood novel. The most rapidly conceived, written, and published of all his novels, *Love among the Cannibals* deals with the two middle-aged members of a second-rate song-writing team, Macgregor and Horter, who pick up a couple of girls and take them to Acapulco for a week of productive work. One is a southern "chick" — Macgregor's Million Dollar Baby who becomes his dimestore bride — and the other is a classic example of the primitive female, Eva by name but to Horter simply "the Greek," who believes that the mind is of the body and who makes Horter share her conviction until he loses her to an aging professor of marine biology, Dr. Leggett. The story is of people who live on each other to the accompaniment of a restless theme song asking "What next?" and it is, in some respects, a zany version of Morris' earlier meditations on the fall of man with an emphasis on sex rather than housekeeping. And throughout the story is the visual symbol of their car — a fireman-red convertible with green leather upholstery and a built-in record player — which is symbolically stripped to its chassis in the way Macgregor and Horter are stripped by their experience, to the "essentials" of the immediate present. *Love among the Cannibals* is the only Morris novel in which the past is apparently judged so inessential that it is completely missing.

Yet Horter's emotion is more profound than any that could surge under the influence of a cardboard moon. Sexual, it is quite different from the casual sexuality which even to Macgregor (a true Hollywood caricature) is less important than the hackneyed sentimentality he considers "the real thing." Horter identified it for what it was while he watched the beginning of Professor Leggett's fall. As Leggett was stuttering with enthusiasm over the "primeval ooze of life" he had fished from the bottom of the sea, Horter observed "that the professor's passion, however platonic in its intentions, had undergone a transformation in the magnetic field of the Greek. His passive ooze had picked up her charge . . . and one fine moment, placing his hand on hers, he would feel the spark. *My child* — he would say, and undergo a shattering development. The sea-green fermenting ooze would not be in his bottle, but in his blood." Horter knew. He saw her as something always "in the process of becoming something else," and whatever he may have contributed to what she called her "development" it was evident, by the end of the book, that she had contributed to his.

It was probably appropriate at this time that Morris should have paused in his career and taken stock of his own aims as a novelist within the mainstream of the American novel. He did so in *The Territory Ahead* (1958), a book of criticism explicitly concerned with the uses and abuses of the past in the light of the immediate present — his obsessed fictional preoccupation. In it he reveals his intense admiration for the perceptive genius and expert craftsmanship of Henry James ("the artist who apprehended much of life without the crippling effects of having lived it") and for the indispensable vitality of D. H. Lawrence's belief that "if life itself could be lived to the full art would grow out of it." Morris reconciled such incongruous admirations through his belief that "If man is nature self-conscious . . . art is his expanding consciousness, and the creative act, in the deepest sense, is his expanding universe." But his own problem was one of the artist who "might well ask how, in such a spinning world as ours, he is to know that he stands in the *present*." "There are no pat answers," he replied, "but there are clues. Since he must live and have his being in a world of clichés, he will know this new world by their absence. He will know it by the fact that he has not been there before. The true territory ahead is what he must imagine for himself. He will recognize it by its strangeness, the lonely pilgrimage through which he attained it, and through the window of his fiction he will breathe the air of his brave new world."

When Morris returned to the Nebraska scene in *Ceremony in Lone Tree* (1960), he actually did present a new world, which had evolved in his earlier books but was now entirely re-created, peopled, and given substance by his imagination. The town of Lone Tree, hardly more than a symbolic name in his earlier novels, was given definite character as a ghost town whose principal inhabitant was Tom Scanlon, a hermit who lived in the past and occupied the abandoned hotel where he had raised the three daughters who were returning with their families for the ceremony of celebrating his ninetieth birthday. Five of the characters from *The Field of Vision* were there: Scanlon himself, Lois (now his oldest rather than his youngest daughter), her husband McKee, their grandson Gordon (now apparently younger than he had been in the earlier book), and Boyd whom McKee had invited in an ill-advised moment. The family was filled out by Maxine, Scanlon's second daughter, with her husband Bud Momeyer and their daughter Etoile, who had her Aunt Lois' beauty but none of her inhibitions. The Momeyers brought with them, though not in person, an awareness of Bud's nephew Lee Roy who had recently used his car to run down and kill two taunting schoolmates and had shared headlines with another boy from the same town who had run wild and killed ten people in an effort to "be somebody." The third daughter, Edna Ewing, was also there with her husband, the caricature of an Oklahoma Colonel, and a ten-thousand-dollar bull pup; and so were two other McKees: young Gordon's older brother, the handsome, horsey, and inarticulate Calvin, and his outspoken mother Eileen. Boyd had picked up en route and brought along for the shock a pathetically young divorcée whom he calls "Daughter" and whose stereotyped swearing gives Etoile a new vocabulary. The same freight that brought them brought a stranger to the group (but not to Morris' readers), Willy Brady, Jr., who had grown up to become an ineffectual writer of Westerns under his middle name Jennings.

Most of the action is comic. The women struggle, in their characteristic ways, with the problems of eating and sleeping under conditions little better than those of camping. Etoile and Calvin "elope" while returning from a neighboring town with a team of mules which they hope will arouse their grandfather out of his half-century of lethargy and take him back to his frontier days. Bud, who has never really grown up, innocently stalks and kills the expensive pup with his bow and arrows. McKee observes Boyd, a still grandiloquent but no longer pathetic failure who seems to have lost even Ty Cobb's pocket — the last relic of his dreams. Lois accidentally fires a revolver from her bedroom window, and that, with the noise of the mules, rouses Scanlon to the memory of his Death Valley adventure: he dies with the old query "That you, Samuels?" on his lips and the expectation of meeting Miss Samantha, his bride. There is no tragedy in Scanlon's death — which, in fact, could be described as a sort of posthumous performance — or in his departure from Lone Tree when a final masterly scene of thoughtless confusion makes plausible the symbolic removal of his remains in the Conestoga wagon in which he was born.

However comic the action and most of the characters in *Ceremony in Lone Tree* might be, the book is loaded with both overtones and undertones of violence. The overtones appear in the formal introduction of Lee Roy into "the roundup" of characters, in the frequent references to the random murderer, and in the constant pretense of shooting by young Gordon. The undertones are introduced by the experience of Boyd, who drives from Mexico to Lone Tree by way of Nevada where an atomic test is scheduled and a tourist camp owner writes after his name on the register "Wake before bomb." No bomb was set off, but the suggestion of an explosion hanging fire pervades the events at Lone Tree. It occurs in the consciousness of all the characters to whom the reader is directly exposed: in the nervous tension of Lois and Maxine, in Boyd's desperate efforts to "clown it up," in McKee's memories and awareness, in Etoile's adolescent sexuality and Calvin's frightened responses, and even in Jennings' haunting recollections of men who played Santa Claus. Morris relieves it by comedy when he has the gentle Bud, playing Indian, kill the bull pup (perhaps the only animal, in any of Morris' novels, which is not sympathetically portrayed) and lets the Ewings get so excited that they rush off to the insurance company with its body instead of taking Scanlon's to the undertaker. There is more tension in *Ceremony in Lone Tree* than in any of the preceding novels: Morris had shucked his Nebraska characters out of the husks of his previous fiction and brought them to renewed life in his imagination.

He did much the same for his post-Nebraska characters in *What a Way to Go* (1962). Its central figure, Arnold Soby, is the same sort of innocuous small-college professor as Foley in *The Huge Season*; and, as in the earlier novel, he is the only character toward whom the author is in any way omniscient. It contains in the person of Miss Winifred Throop the domineering female of the Pennsylvania novels, this time in the role in which Morris had discovered her in real life — that of headmistress of a fashionable girl's school, though here retired, out of her native habitat, and considerably less sure of herself. It also includes a host of the grotesques Morris likes to observe and mimic: Miss Kollwitz, an avid peeler of fruit, who was a teacher of modern languages and Miss Throop's companion and protector; Mr. Lipari, pickling himself in brandy while he crossed the Atlantic for an audience with the Pope; Signor Condotti-Pignata, who wanted to be another Botticelli but had either too much or too little imagination to succeed; Dr. Hodler, the pompous Swiss-German professor of classics; the dwarfish and impish Austrian Herr Perkheimer, who was going to rescue Greece from generations of photographic ash by shooting new scenes with unloaded cameras; a flock of German *Wandervogel*, led by the efficient Fraulein Kretschmar and the giant Herr Holzapfel with a baby face and the mind of an arrested adolescent; and a score or more of incidental characters, all vividly captured in caricature. Finally there is the equivalent of "the Greek" in *Love among the Cannibals* — a real one in Professor Soby's memory of his short marriage to a young bride, and a potential one in the person of the seventeen-year-old Cynthia, Miss Throop's niece and the Galatea of every man's Pygmalion. Awkwardly outgrowing her clothes, devoted to popsicles, with bands on her teeth, Cynthia was nevertheless Primavera to Signor Pignata, Nausicaa to Professor Hodler, Fraulein Liebfraumilch to Perkheimer, and a terror to Herr Holzapfel. To Soby she was, in one respect, a familiar experience of his life as a college professor and, in another, a crucial challenge to his literary imagination.

For Soby — sane, safe, considerate Soby — had depths beyond the depths revealed by Peter Foley. His strange captivity was to Thomas Mann's *Death in Venice* because his young Greek bride had enabled him to understand the bacchanal of Aschenbach's dream and to recognize a profound wisdom beneath the morbid symbols of German romanticism. He hoped to express it in his own way in a book on "the wisdom of the body" but had no conscious notion of what such wisdom was. It was not sexual violence, which he had experienced, but something as imaginative in its way as was Aschenbach's infatuation with Tadzio. Perhaps it was of the spinal cord ("That living root that connected the brain of man with his primeval tail") or of the eye itself which had "a small brain of its own . . . a tiny bud of the brain . . . attached to the back of it" where "the visible world was made visible." Soby, like Foley, had apparently read Darwin, who had said (in a sentence Morris used as an epigraph for the book), "I remember well the time when the thought of the eye made me cold all over." But Soby was not a scientist devoted to impersonal rationality. He was a humanist who suspected that "the wisdom of the body counselled the brain what to feel and think," that it might be "the source of fiction, as well as what were known as facts." Cynthia stimulated it. Soby did not lust for her. On the contrary, she reminded him "of the Virgin's silver beauty/ All fish below the thighs." When he looked at her, he saw something "out of this world" — "far out" — and was drawn to her more mysteriously than Aschenbach had been drawn to Tadzio. He made her — or she made herself — his bride.

Although it is one of the most richly and exaggeratedly comic of all Morris' books, *What a Way to Go* treats seriously the problem of reality. Cynthia Pomeroy was a carefully calculated representation of the type of character toward which he had been groping with Agee Ward and Charles Lawrence. Easy enough to sketch in caricature, she was impossible to paint or to direct in the pageant of Nausicaa receiving Ulysses because she was in the unstable process of change (as Soby so clearly realized) and such stability as she possessed existed in the eyes of the beholder who tried to fit her into the pattern of whatever dream he most cherished. But she could not be frozen in a cliché or become a bee in amber. The only thing that one could be sure of was that she was alive. She represented the primitive force which produced a drive toward the unknown. Reality was to be found, fleetingly, somewhere along the way. Soby realized this and, with the wisdom of the body, clutched at it. But what he caught we are never told. For *What a Way to Go* raised a question which could be answered negatively but not, in any permanent sense, positively. One of Cynthia's realities might have been captured in Signor Pignata's painting had he ever been able to settle upon the way to paint her. It could not have been captured in a photograph of the Nausicaa pageant Dr. Hodler tried to stage. She was a stimulus to the creative eye rather than an artifact for the eye of the camera, and her reality was to be found in her effect. Like the characters in *Ceremony in Lone Tree,* who are more fully realized than those of *The Home Place,* she has more reality in the novel than she could ever have in most people's lives.

In *Ceremony in Lone Tree* and *What a Way to Go,* Morris apparently found his creative inspiration in the attempt to do for himself what he had attempted to have his characters do in *The Field of Vision* — to gather up the durable fragments of his experience and come to imaginative terms with them. The first novel was an imaginative reconstruction of his actual and creative association with Nebraska; the second, with those of his more recent experiences in the East and in Europe. But he had other business with his personal past which he had to settle before he could exorcise it from the dominant and almost obsessive position it had held for two decades in his imagination. This was with the period from early 1930 through the middle of 1934 which included the months he had spent on his uncle's ranch in the Texas panhandle, his college years, and his *Wanderjahr* in Europe. He came to grips with it in *Cause for Wonder* (1963).

He did it through the mind of Warren Howe, a middle-aged writer who thirty years before had passed four months in strange captivity (as Morris himself had) to an ancient castle and its mad owner in the Austrian Alps. Howe received an invitation to the madman's funeral and in seeking a companion for the trip brought this period of Morris' life to a focus upon the most haunting part of it. He first sought out his Texas uncle, Fremont Osborn, in a chapter which provides the context for many of the "spots of time" scattered through Morris' other novels; and then approached a former college friend, Charles Horney, in another chapter which may explain why Morris took off for Europe instead of taking a degree. Finally he persuaded Sol Spiegel, a Santa Monica junk dealer and his former companion on a bicycle trip through Italy, to accompany him on what was to prove another strange adventure.

Although the book is divided into two sections, the first called "Time Present" and the second "Time Past," it actually presents a continuous narrative; and the time division refers to the focal point of Howe's awareness, calling attention to Morris' use of a movie-camera technique which enables him to zoom in on something distant in time in a way that was impossible with the still-camera technique of *The Home Place* or the use of narrative juxtaposition in *The Huge Season*. In the continuity of the story Howe and Spiegel arrive at Schloss Riva to find the Meister, Monsieur Etienne Dulac, very much alive and the finest human symbol of "sublime audacity" in any of Morris' novels. He had himself been responsible for sending out the invitations and had succeeded in rounding up two other people from Howe's past, Wolfgang Prutscher and Katherine Brownell, for the fantastic events of twenty-four hours during which "George" (the Till Eulenspiegel of the castle roofs) scatters white paint as he had once scattered snow and the seventy-five-year-old crippled Meister slides down a mountainside and dies peacefully in bed — the last and possibly planned eccentricity of a long career devoted to giving other people cause for wonder.

The events of the twenty-four hours, however, are less real to Howe than those evoked from the past, some of them a part of Morris' own experience and some of them his imaginings of what the Meister might have done had he maintained his characteristic audacity through World War II. The reality in the book is of a sort that could be better appreciated by Arnold Soby than by any but its most sensitive readers: something to be found, fleetingly, somewhere along the way of eternal change as the past is being transformed into the future. Dulac was more real than Scanlon because he had more to pass on — an audacity which would continue to lead a life of its own — and a recipient better conceived for that purpose than Gordon McKee had been. The recipient was Katherine's grandson Brian, a child prodigy shaped like Uncle Dudley; and the greatest cause for Howe's wonder during the whole fantastic day was the relationship between him and the old man. As Dulac placed his hand on Brian's head "Howe sensed the flow of an alternating current. The past into the present, the present into the past. . . . From the old, the charge was now being passed to the new. *What* charge? That was what one never knew. The new, unused heads, like empty deep-freeze cartons, would not give up their meaning — if it could be said they had one — until thawed. The present would prove to be whatever proved unexpendable. Good or bad. If it existed it had proved itself. . . . As a pallbearer, the boy carried the future, or nothing at all."

Cause for Wonder is the most difficult of Morris' books because it is (with the possible exception of *The Works of Love*) the most private and because it required the most complex technique to come to imaginative terms with the durable experiences on which it was based — so durable, in fact, that the published book represented his fifth attempt to deal with them over a period of twenty-six years. More completely concerned with the author's individual past than either of the other two novels of the early sixties, it also brought him closer to a concern for the future; and, in doing so, it marked the culmination of another major stage in his literary development. The two which were to follow were to be free from the signs of struggle with his own past which had marked his work for two decades. Better than any of his other novels, they were to show where he stood in the uncertain and insecure present.

One Day (1965) not only marks the release of Morris' field of vision from those spots of time which attracted it toward his own past but displays the full development of a fictional technique which enabled him to bring into almost perfect balance the two qualities which distinguish him among modern American novelists: the extraordinary range of knowledge and sympathetic understanding he can apply to the representation of human beings in the infinite variety of their comic humors, and the seriousness and honesty of his search for meaning and hope in a world that so many of his contemporaries have been content to present as absurd.

The technique he uses is that of achieving intensity by means of the classical unities of time and place. In several of his earlier novels he had confined the action to the events of a single day, and in most of these he had kept it close enough to a single place to allow his characters to move from scene to scene plausibly within his time pattern. In all of them, however, he had increased the range of his story by using such devices as the interpolated manuscript (in *The Huge Season*) and individually labeled points of view which allowed him to present not only the awareness but (as in *The Field of Vision*) the memories of his various characters. In *One Day*, however, he observed the unities with a more-than-classic strictness by keeping the action between pre-dawn

34

and midnight in the small northern California town of Escondido and consistently focusing it upon the animal pound in the town's center; and he achieved a greater unity of effect by telling his story (and the stories of his individual characters) from the consistent point of view of an omniscient novelist. The day was November 22, 1963, but Morris avoided any journalistic exploitation of President Kennedy's assassination. He presented it as a day of "such unspeakable human folly" as to raise the question whether mankind should follow the pattern of its own civilization or take Whitman's advice to "turn and live with animals" because they bring better "tokens" — however mysterious in their origin — of man's self.

The pattern of questionable civilization is set by Evelina Cartwright who dominates the town with her loud voice and hearty manner, her tourist gift shop, her high-class animal pound, and her strange collection of protégés: Luigi Boni, the Venetian barber and her pet artist; the Yucatanian dog-catcher, Ignacio Chavez; the hard-of-hearing superintendent of the pound, Wendell Horlick, with his frustrated wife and grasping son Irving; and the astrologist and fortune-teller, Adele Skopje, who is hardly conscious of anything in the present. Its promise of the future is to be found in the person of Evelina's childlike daughter Alec, who has been a freedom rider in the Deep South and has brought home her illegitimate mulatto child and secretly deposited it in the pound as a gesture of protest. She innocently believed this would shake the world until she became disillusioned by the ability of her mother and everybody else to take the gesture in full stride — just as most of them could take the assassination of the President.

The question of turning away from the pattern of civilization is raised in the mind of the local veterinarian, Harold Cowie, because he is worried about the modern necessity for "giving up" in order to survive: "Cowie had given up people, Alec had given up her child, numberless lovers had given up love, and increasing numbers had given up their conscious lives. A non-conscious life they still lived, and the future looked bright for non-conscious dying. But to be fully conscious was to be fully exposed. . . . As a matter of survival one gave it up. At one and the same moment this was an act of salvation and an act of destruction."

In giving up, one might give up to many things; and it was in giving himself up to an American archetype that the President's assassin, by implication in Cowie's mind, became a member of the Escondido community. He was, in his way, like Evelina and Alec: "In representing nothing bigger than himself, Lee Oswald represented more than enough. He did in Texas. He did in all of America. A free man, he testified to the horrible burden of freedom: how connect with some*thing*? How relate to some*one*? It was no accident that he singled out the man who represented the maximum of human connections, and displaced this man, this symbol of connections, with himself. Lee Oswald had merely deprived another man of what, in his opinion, he had been deprived: the right to the pursuit and possession of happiness. As an American it was not necessary for him to speak for others: his life and happiness depended on his speaking for himself. His life, and as it so often happened, another man's death."

Alec had been right in her desperate cry: "I did it. We all did it." For, Morris had continued through Cowie's chain of thought, "This senseless crime not only made history: it made American sense. In each American ear the word from Dallas would acquire its own troubled burden of meaning, and its own intolerable burden of meaninglessness. What word was it? How well Cowie knew it. *Impotence.* The assurance that nothing said, nothing written or cabled, nothing accepted or rejected, nothing suffered or felt, nothing now up before Congress or still in the blueprints, nothing dug out of the past or prescribed for the future, would restore to a man his belief in his power to affect the course of human events. He might exert it, but believe in it he did not."

This was all the wisdom of the mind that could be brought to bear on the tragedy. The wisdom of the body had nothing to offer. Conchita, the wife of Chavez, and Dora, the wife of Luigi, possessed it and were able to grieve passionately during the day and sleep peacefully through the night; but their husbands lay awake with thoughts of death or frustration. The thoughts of the sleepless American women were, like those of Alec, "of no moment." Cowie's sleepless thoughts, however, were. Though impotence in its extremity could make a man "murderously potent," most people could not act but, like Alec, merely protest; and his nightmare was of "what might happen anywhere under the sign of impotence": of some "day without end" when "impotence and protest would lie down in darkness, like lovers, and issue from that union would turn up in Dallas, in Escondido, and in towns yet to be heard from. . . . Where such lovers lay down, such issue would turn up. In one voice they would cry for Havoc, in another for Help. Whoever told it this would prove to be a story as strange, or stranger than that of Lee Oswald, common as the air that bathed the globe, inscrutable as death. An American story. No matter who told it, that's what it would be."

Such a novel as this would be profoundly pessimistic were it not filled with Morris' fascination with life. He may not have approved of Escondido and its more aggressive inhabitants, but he appreciated it in all its details and prized them in all their peculiarities: the managing Evelina and the frustrated Miriam Horlick, Adele Skopje, the movie-type sheriff, the friendly owner of the liquor store, and Cowie with whom he shared a few remaining specks of time. He obviously delighted in his oddball characters, the Chavez and Boni families, and the people who

37

came into the novel through their and Alec's and Cowie's memories; and he took a sardonic delight in the portrayal of the broad-bottomed Irving, who was bound to succeed in Escondido, and of "Protest" Jackson who was equally bound to succeed in the mass-media coverage of freedom riders. He also made the animals fascinating: Evelina's neurotic and Cowie's antisocial cat, and especially the hound Larkspur who fell in love with Wendell Horlick in Pennsylvania and crossed the continent with him, sitting erect in a rumble seat, wearing motorcycle goggles and a hat with ribbons under her chin, and perhaps audaciously enjoying life as a girl until she got to Escondido and went to pieces when she discovered what it was really like to escape a dog's life.

The imaginative richness and vitality of *One Day* is much more powerful than its intellectual despair, and it was an expression of Morris' faith as a novelist: he must be true to the present in which he lives, even though the implications of that present may be tragically inscrutable to the intellect. But so long as the creative imagination exists and finds substance to feed its energy something will come out of it. One might like to play with the fancy that nature should make a new beginning with a chipmunk, a cat, or a dog, but he knows that man has the head start. Man's capacity for tenderness (to which Eiseley attributed human survival) as well as the infinite variety of his oddities is unmatched in the animal world, and if he can come to imaginative terms with his eccentricities he may find in them the necessary compensation for his follies. The effort to do this has been the emerging figure in the carpet of Wright Morris' fiction.

It seems obvious from *One Day* that Morris could imagine no possible shock to the rational mind that might disturb the normal tenor of existence in a small town where people have withdrawn into live oddity or deadendedness, giving up consciousness, as he put it, in the interest of survival. But what of the irrational force of life itself? Morris has not yet been willing to speculate upon what it might lead to in the future, but he has always been willing, joyously if somewhat sardonically, to affirm and demonstrate its existence. Nowhere has he or anyone else done so more entertainingly than in the latest and most perfect of his short novels, *In Orbit* (1967).

The setting is the small Indiana town of Pickett, and the irrational forces which strike it in another single day are represented by an American teen-age high school dropout and an erratic type of cyclone known as a "twister." Jubal Gainer is on his way to be inducted into the Army when he suddenly finds that his world is too much with him and takes off on a stolen motorcycle, runs out of gas, and creates havoc in the town. He attempts to rape the feebleminded "Miss Holly" Stohrmeyer (who thinks, from his helmet, that she has been visited by a spaceman) and stirs her guardian, Sanford Avery, and the local newspaper editor, Curt Hodler, in an unexpected way by his act. He pushes a bag of cherries over the head of odd little Professor Haffner and sends him to the hospital. He rewards Oscar Kashperl's talent for divining the unknown by stabbing him. He politely rescues Charlotte Hatfield when she catches her shoe in a grating and rebuffs her efforts at further acquaintance yet watches from the darkness as she dances while the cyclone rips the roof off the house. And at the end, he rides away with her shoes in his helmet. The cyclone, with all its death and destruction, will probably fade into the memory of other storms long before Jubal Gainer ceases to be remembered as another man who was there.

But the relative effect of these two natural forces is irrelevant. Morris is no longer concerned with the past but the present. And the present is in Jubal rather than in the people he leaves behind. He rides away, low in the saddle, "like a diver who has gone too deep and too long without air." Before him lies "the sunrise on the windows of the Muncie Draft Board" and perhaps the plains of China: "There is no place to hide. But perhaps the important detail escapes you. He is in motion. Now you see him, now you don't. If you pin him down in time he is lost in space. Somewhere between where he is from and where he is going he wheels in an unpredictable orbit. He is as free, and as captive, as the wind in his face . . . the rain-scoured light gleams on his helmet, like a saucer in orbit, where the supernatural is just naturally a part of his life."

Although Morris was writing about a particular character — a juvenile delinquent who looked like a spaceman and acted like a bull in a china shop, violent but not vicious — he could have found no better words to express his conception of the role of the artist in modern life. There should be no place (as he had made clear in his comments on T. S. Eliot in *The Territory Ahead*) for him to hide. He should be in motion, wheeling in an unpredictable orbit somewhere between where he is from and where he is going, something mysterious and inexplicable, perhaps, but just naturally a part of life. That he himself should have been able to play that role for more than a quarter of a century is his most remarkable achievement.

The conception of the artist which Morris has formed and followed, however, has created an obstacle to his reception by the public. His refusal to accept the traditional form of the novel which focuses attention upon the adventures of a central character (a hero or heroine of one sort or another) has bewildered the professionally rapid readers who have found his books as perplexing as they found those of the early Faulkner. On the other hand, the newer variety of critics have been put off by his Jamesian insistence upon the artist's role as the man who was there as a creative, affective intelligence which refuses either to be pinned down or evaded. It is the artist, Morris insists, whose vision counts. It is he, rather than the reader, who should be in orbit.

An awareness of his detachment from the successful exploiters of mass media is evident in his recent troubled book of criticism, *A Bill of Rites, a Bill of Wrongs, a Bill of Goods* (1968). More concerned with the social than the literary scene and filled with "laughter at what ceases to amuse," it contains a chapter on "Reflections on the Death of the Reader" which meditates upon the professional reviewer whose function is to make reading unnecessary, the machine-trained reader who can go through an "average" novel in an hour, and the "overtrained, symbol-haunted reader" who can take no pleasure in the elusiveness of a living thing but must pin it to a board in order to categorize it. "A different level of consciousness," Morris says, "seems to be engaged in the student who is studying *The Sound and the Fury,* and the reader, however naïve, who settles down with nothing but the book." The reader whose passing he mourns is the one willing to settle down with nothing but a receptive mind and a book: "Until a dialogue exists between the writer and this reader, on terms established by the author, a book is powerless to speak, or persuade, or do more than level a tipping table."

Can such a dialogue exist in the modern world of mass media, instant communication, pop art, and audience participation? Has the world become nothing more than "A Museum of Happenings"? This is the question which troubles him, especially as it is raised by the existence of artists who do not believe in art, by "the writer's misgiving, in theory and practice, of the ultimate truth of imagination," and by the creative critic who turns every work of art into "the raw material for an endless series of appropriations." *A Bill of Rites* is an angry book by a man who has devoted his life to the claims of the imagination and has had his claims pre-empted by psychedelic dropouts or disallowed by such superficial doubletalk as "the media is the message."

But it is a book which faces the practical dilemma of the serious imaginative writer in the present. Should he give up, in the interest of survival, his sense of his own uniqueness and address himself to "creative" readers who have learned to make raw material out of art? Or should he insist upon the artist's peculiar power to transform the raw material of reality into something that Keats had called "the truth of Imagination"? Morris revealed his own position when he commented on "a student of the modern novel" who had recently asked him — "off the cuff and man to man" — if he didn't think the trapped fly in one of his books was "a symbolic cliché": "The Midwest setting of this novel," he said, "simply buzzed with trapped flies, and so did the book. They were flies when they came to my mind and they were still flies when I put them on the page. . . . That they might also prove to be symbols was not my proper business. When the writing is good everything is symbolic, but symbolic writing is seldom good. Symbol hunting is the fashionable safari for the vacationing writer and reader — a way of killing time."

Such a statement may be extreme, but it represents the stand of a responsible novelist against the "liquidation" of art by "an endless series" of critical or even schoolboyish "appropriations." The responsibility of the novelist which Morris asserts is that of accepting the real world and bringing it into a field of vision which will give it meaning. The meaning will be imaginative and suggestive rather than rational and reductive. If the suggestion is powerful enough it will stir the imagination of the reader, induce him to share the author's vision, and to that extent become symbolic. But the controlling power will be the mind of the writer, not that of the reader. The artist may be in the category of a neurotic chipmunk, a placid transvestite, a host at his own funeral, or a dog who thinks she is human; but without the sub-lime audacity of his creative imagination the world will degen-erate into a museum of happenings in which the past is unknown and the future nonexistent.

In developing and following this creed, Morris has worked and reworked the raw material of his experience into a fictional real-ity which has a life — and a potentiality for future existence — of its own. And in doing so he has, in the words of one of his most recent and perspective critics, made "the novel seem brand new again." The newness is genuine. Morris must be taken on his own terms or not at all. But the terms have been more thought-fully developed and established in practice for a longer time than those of any other American novelist writing today. What he asks his readers to take is an artist's effort to reconcile the truth of fact with the truth of imagination and "make it new." His own unique medium is the high seriousness of brilliant comedy in which the absurd is laid bare without bitterness and perhaps with as much faith in the past and hope for the future as a sensi-tive and well-informed intellectual in modern America can manage.

✗ Selected Bibliography

Works of Wright Morris

BOOKS (FIRST AMERICAN, PAPERBACK, AND FOREIGN EDITIONS)

My Uncle Dudley. New York: Harcourt, Brace, 1942.

The Man Who Was There. New York: Scribner's, 1945.

The Inhabitants. New York: Scribner's, 1946. (Photographs and text.)

The Home Place. New York: Scribner's, 1948. (Photographs and text.)

The World in the Attic. New York: Scribner's, 1949.

Man and Boy. New York: Knopf, 1951. London: Gollancz, 1952. *Il padre dell'eroe*. Turin: Einaudi, 1954.

The Works of Love. New York: Knopf, 1952.

The Deep Sleep. New York: Scribner's, 1953. London: Eyre and Spottiswoode, 1954. *Die Gläserne Insel*. Stuttgart: Goverts, 1957. Frankfurt: Fischer Bücherei, 1960. Augsburg: Bibliothek Suhrkamp, 1967. *Un Sonno Profondo*. Milan: Arnoldo Mondadori Editore, 1961.

The Huge Season. New York: Viking Press, 1954. London: Secker and Warburg, 1955. *Die Masslose Zeit*. Stuttgart: Goverts, 1958.

The Field of Vision. New York: Harcourt, Brace, 1956. New York: New American Library (Signet), 1957. London: Weidenfeld and Nicolson, 1957.

Love among the Cannibals. New York: Harcourt, Brace, 1957. New York: New American Library (Signet), 1958. London: Weidenfeld and Nicolson, 1958. *Amore tra i Cannibali*. Milan: Feltrinelli, 1958, 1961; Garzanti, 1966. *Liebe unter Kannibalen*. Stuttgart: Goverts, 1959. Frankfurt: Fischer Bücherei, 1962. *O Amor Entre Canibais*. Rio de Janiero: Casa Editoa Vecchi, n.d.

The Territory Ahead. New York: Harcourt, Brace, 1958. New York: Atheneum, paperback, 1963. (Essays.)

Ceremony in Lone Tree. New York: Atheneum, 1960. New York: New American Library (Signet), 1962. London: Weidenfeld and Nicolson, 1961. *Unterwegs nach Lone Tree*. Munich: Piper Verlag, 1962. *La Dernière Fête*. Paris: Gallimard, 1964. *Ceremonia en Lone Tree*. Buenos Aires: Plaza and Janes, 1967.

What a Way to Go. New York: Atheneum, 1962. *Miss Nausikaa*. Munich: Piper Verlag, 1964.

The Mississippi Reader. Garden City, N.Y.: Doubleday (Anchor), 1962. (An anthology, edited by Morris.)

Cause for Wonder. New York: Atheneum, 1963.

One Day. New York: Atheneum, 1965.

In Orbit. New York: New American Library, 1967; Signet edition, 1968.

A Bill of Rites, a Bill of Wrongs, a Bill of Goods. New York: New American Library, 1968. (Essays.)

SHORT STORIES

"Ram in the Thicket," *Harper's Bazaar*, 82:133, 182–94 (May 1948). Reprinted in the *National Book Award Reader*. New York: Popular Library, 1966. Also reprinted in *Contemporary American Short Stories*, edited by D. and S. Angus. New York: Fawcett, 1967.

"Where's Justice?" in *Cross Section, 1948*, edited by Edwin Seaver. New York: Simon and Schuster, 1948. Pp. 221–30.

"A Man of Caliber," *Kenyon Review*, 11:101–7 (Winter 1949).

"The Lover," *Harper's Bazaar*, 83:118, 175–80 (May 1949).

"The Sound Tape," *Harper's Bazaar*, 85:125, 175–77 (May 1951).

"The Character of the Lover," *American Mercury*, 73:43–49 (August 1951).

"The Rites of Spring," in *New World Writing*, No. 1. New York: New American Library, 1952. Pp. 140–45.

"The Safe Place," *Kenyon Review*, 16:597–600 (Autumn 1954).

"The Word from Space — A Story," *Atlantic Monthly*, 201:38–42 (April 1958). Reprinted in *Magazine of Science Fiction*, 15:111–18 (September 1958).

"The Cat in the Picture . . ." *Esquire*, 49:90–94 (May 1958).

"Wake before Bomb," *Esquire*, 52:311–15 (December 1959).

"Love, Is That You?" *Esquire*, 65:70, 132–36 (March 1966).

ESSAYS

"The New Criticism," *American Scholar*, 20:359 (Summer 1951).

"The Violent Land — Faulkner and Expressionism," *Magazine of Art*, 45:99–103 (March 1952).

"How Come You Settled Down Here?" *Vogue*, 119:117–19 (April 1952).

"Norman Rockwell's America," *Atlantic Monthly*, 200:133–38 (December 1957).

"The Territory Ahead," in *The Living Novel: A Symposium*, edited by Granville Hicks. New York: Macmillan, 1957. Pp. 120–56.

"Our Endless Plains," *Holiday*, 24:68–69, 138–43 (July 1958).

"Henry James's *The American Scene*," *Texas Quarterly*, 1:27–42 (Summer–Autumn 1958).

"The Cars in My Life," *Holiday*, 24:43–53 (December 1958).

"The Ability to Function: A Reappraisal of Fitzgerald and Hemingway," in *New World Writing*, No. 13. New York: New American Library, 1958. Pp. 34–51.

"Mexican Journey," *Holiday*, 26:50–63 (November 1959).

"Nature before Darwin," *Esquire*, 52:64–70 (November 1959).

"Lawrence and the Immediate Present," in *A D. H. Lawrence Miscellany*, edited by Harry T. Moore. Carbondale: Southern Illinois Press, 1959. Pp. 7–12. Reprinted from *The Territory Ahead*.

"The Open Road," *Esquire*, 53:98–99 (June 1960).

"Made in U.S.A.," *American Scholar*, 29:483–94 (Autumn 1960).

"One Law for the Lion," *Partisan Review*, 28:541–51 (May–June 1961).

"Conversations in a Small Town," *Holiday*, 30:98, 100, 103, 107, 108 (November 1961).

"Shooting the Works," *Partisan Review*, 4:578–86 (Fall 1962).

"The Function of Nostalgia," in *F. Scott Fitzgerald: A Collection of Critical Essays*, edited by Arthur Mizener. New York: Prentice-Hall, 1963. Pp. 25–31.

"Death of the Reader," *Nation*, 198:53–54 (January 13, 1964).

Foreword to Mark Twain's *Pudd'nhead Wilson*. New York: New American Library (Signet), 1964.

Afterword to R. H. Dana's *Two Years before the Mast*. New York: New American Library (Signet), 1964.

"Letter to a Young Critic," *Massachusetts Review*, 6 (No. 1):93–100 (Autumn–Winter 1964–65).

Introduction to Sherwood Anderson's *Windy McPherson's Son*. Chicago: University of Chicago Press, 1965.

"The Lunatic, the Lover, and the Poet," *Kenyon Review*, 27:727–37 (Autumn 1965).

"The Origin of a Species, 1942–1957," *Massachusetts Review*, 7(No. 1):121–35 (Winter 1966).

"How Things Are," in *Arts and the Public*, edited by James E. Miller and Paul D. Herring. Chicago: University of Chicago Press, 1967. Pp. 33–52; see also pp. 230–53 *passim*.

PHOTOGRAPHS AND PHOTO-TEXTS

"The Inhabitants," in *New Directions in Prose and Poetry, 1940*, edited by James Laughlin. Norfolk, Conn.: New Directions, 1940. Pp. 145–80.

"White House," *Twice a Year*, 5–6:116 (Fall–Winter 1940 and Spring–Summer 1941, double issue).

"The Inhabitants," *Direction*, 3:12–13 (November 1940).

"Landscape with Figures," in *New Directions in Prose and Poetry, 1941*, edited by James Laughlin. Norfolk, Conn.: New Directions, 1941. Pp. 253–77.

"The Inhabitants," *Photography* (London), July–August 1947, pp. 26–29.

"The Inhabitants," in *Spearhead: An Anthology*. Norfolk, Conn.: New Directions, 1947. Pp. 191–201.

"The American Scene," *New York Times Magazine*, July 4, 1948, pp. 14–15.

"An Author Remembers His Home Place in Nebraska," *Life*, 25:8–10 (July 26, 1948).

Selected Bibliography

"Home Town Revisited," *New York Times Magazine*, April 24, 1949, pp. 24–25.

"The World in the Attic," *Photography* (London), September 1949, pp. 17–26.

"Summer Encore," *New York Times Magazine*, November 13, 1949, pp. 26–27.

"Built with More Than Hands," *New York Times Magazine*, December 25, 1949, pp. 12–13.

"Guest of Honour — No. 12 — Wright Morris (U.S.A.)," *Photography* (London), July 1949, pp. 14–15.

"The Home: Echoes from Empty Houses," in *The Nation's Heritage*, Vol. 1, No. 3 (1949), no pagination (24 photographs).

U.S. Camera Annual, 1949, edited by Tom Maloney. New York: U.S. Camera Corp., 1949. P. 30.

"Out of Shoes Come New Feet," *New York Times Magazine*, June 11, 1950, pp. 20–21.

"Privacy as a Subject for Photography," *Magazine of Art*, 44:51–55 (February 1951).

Bio-Bibliographical Material

The basic checklist of Morris' publications from 1942 to 1961 is by Stanton J. Linden and David Madden in *Critique*, 4(No. 3):77–87 (Winter 1961–62). It also lists reviews of his books, sources of biographical information, and critical comments. This has been supplemented and brought up to 1963 by Madden in his full-length critical study, *Wright Morris*, pp. 177–84, which omits the reviews but provides valuable annotations for all Morris' shorter pieces and for the secondary material. This "Selected Bibliography" only adds recent titles and does not supersede the two on which it is based. Additional bio-bibliographical information may be found throughout *The Territory Ahead* and the essays listed above. The dust jacket for *The Field of Vision* provides a valuable comment on that book by the author, and "Comments by Wright Morris" are included in Granville Hicks's excellent review of *Ceremony in Lone Tree* in *Saturday Review*, 43:11 (July 9, 1960).

Bleufarb, Sam. "Point of View: An Interview with Wright Morris," *Accent*, 19:34–46 (Winter 1959).

Breit, Harvey. "Talk with Wright Morris," *New York Times Book Review*, June 10, 1951, p. 19.

Busch, Arthur J. "Fellowships for Photography," *Popular Photography*, 2:22–23, 82 (October 1942).

Hutchins, John K. "On an Author," *New York Herald Tribune Book Review*, June 3, 1951, p. 2.

Kuehl, John, ed. *Write and Rewrite*. New York: Meredith Press, 1967. Published in paperback as *Creative Writing and Rewriting*. New York: Appleton-Century-Crofts, 1967. Pp. 98–129.

LEON HOWARD

Kunitz, Stanley J., ed. "Wright Morris," *Twentieth Century Authors*, First Supplement. New York: H. W. Wilson, 1955. Pp. 691–92.

"Main Line Author of the Month," *Main Line*, June 1951, pp. 24, 41–42.

Warfel, Harry R. *American Novelists of Today*. New York: American Book, 1951. P. 312.

"Wright Morris in Oberlin," *Plum Creek Review* (Oberlin College, Ohio), Spring 1965. (Interview.)

Critical Studies

Allen, Walter. *The Modern Novel in Britain and the United States*. New York: Dutton, 1964. Pp. 315–17.

Baumbach, Jonathan. "Wake before Bomb: *Ceremony in Lone Tree*," *Critique*, 4:56–71 (Winter 1961–62). See also *The Landscape of Nightmare*. New York: New York University Press, 1965. Pp. 152–69.

Booth, Wayne C. "The Two Worlds in the Fiction of Wright Morris," *Sewanee Review*, 65:375–99 (Summer 1957).

———. "The Shaping of Prophecy: Craft and Idea in the Novels of Wright Morris," *American Scholar*, 31:608–26 (Autumn 1962).

Carpenter, Frederic. "Wright Morris and the Territory Ahead," *College English*, 21:147–56 (December 1959).

Eisinger, Chester E. *Fiction of the Forties*. Chicago: University of Chicago Press, 1963. Pp. 328–41.

Fiedler, Leslie. *Love and Death in the American Novel*. New York: Criterion Books, 1960. Pp. 323–24, 471–72.

Garrett, George P. "Morris the Magician: A Look at *In Orbit*," *Hollins Critic* (Hollins College, Virginia), Vol. 4, No. 3 (June 1967).

Hassan, Ihab. *Radical Innocence: Studies in the Contemporary American Novel*. Princeton, N.J.: Princeton University Press, 1961; New York: Harper and Row, 1966. Pp. 6, 78, 101.

Hunt, John W., Jr. "The Journey Back: The Early Novels of Wright Morris," *Critique*, 5:41–60 (Spring–Summer 1962).

Klein, Marcus. *After Alienation*. Cleveland and New York: World, 1964. Pp. 196–246.

Madden, David. "The Hero and the Witness in Wright Morris' Field of Vision," *Prairie Schooner*, 34:263–78 (Fall 1960).

———. "The Great Plains in the Novels of Wright Morris," *Critique*, 4:5–23 (Winter 1961–62).

———. *Wright Morris*. New York: Twayne, 1964.

Trachtenberg, Alan. "The Craft of Vision," *Critique*, 4:41–55 (Winter 1961–62).

Waterman, Arthur E. "The Novels of Wright Morris: An Escape from Nostalgia," *Critique*, 4:24–40 (Winter 1961–62).

48